MUMMIES MADE IN EGYPT

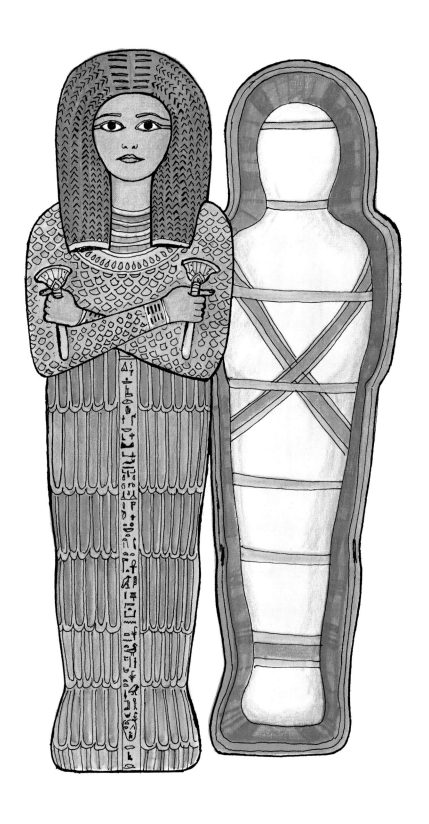

MUMMIES
MADE IN EGYPT

written and illustrated by

ALIKI

HarperCollinsPublishers

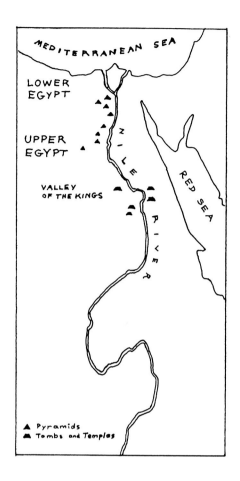

ANCIENT EGYPT was a long, narrow country
divided in half by the Nile River. Food was grown along
the fertile banks of the river. The land beyond was desert.
There the ancient Egyptians buried their dead.

Mummies Made in Egypt
Copyright © 1979 by Aliki Brandenberg
Manufactured in China. All rights reserved.
For information address HarperCollins Children's Books,
a division of HarperCollins Publishers,
10 East 53rd Street, New York, NY 10022.

Library of Congress Cataloging in Publication Data
Aliki.
    Mummies made in Egypt.
    Describes the techniques and reasons for the use of
mummification in ancient Egypt.
        1. Mummies—Juvenile Literature.   [1. Mummies.
2. Egypt—Antiquities.]   I. Title.
DT62.M7A43   393'.3'0932   77-26603
ISBN 0-690-03858-5
ISBN 0-690-03859-3 (lib. bdg.)

    (A Harper trophy book)
ISBN 0-06-446011-8   85-42746

FOR BARBARA FENTON

Special thanks to Franz, Jason and Alexa for their
advice and patience, and to Dr. Robert S. Bianchi,
Adjunct Assistant Professor of Egyptian Art,
New York University, for his generous help.

Some of the gods and goddesses of the dead.

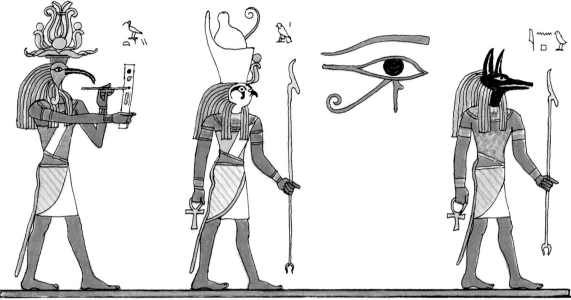

THOTH	HORUS	UDJAT	ANUBIS
Ibis-headed God of Scribes	God of the Sky, son of Osiris	Magic Eye of Horus, Protector of the Dead	Jackal-headed God of Embalmers

GEB	HATHOR	ISIS	NEPHTHYS
God of Earth	Goddess of the city of Dendera	Wife of Osiris, mother of Horus	Sister of Isis

TEFNUT	SHU	RE-HORAKHTY
Goddess of Moisture	God of Air	Horus of the Two Horizons

OSIRIS

Prince of the Dead, God of the Underworld

The ancient Egyptians had one great wish.
That wish was to live forever.
Egyptians believed that after they died a new life began.
They would live in their tombs as they lived on earth.
They would also travel to another world to live with
   gods and goddesses of the dead.

Egyptians believed everyone had a ba, or soul,
    and a ka, an invisible twin of the person.

The ba was represented as
a bird with a human head.

The dead person and his ka.

They believed that when a person died, his ba and ka
    were released from his body and lived on in the tomb.
The ba would keep contact with the living family
    and friends of the dead.
The ka traveled back and forth from the body
    to the other world.

In order for a person to live forever, the ba and ka
    had to be able to recognize the body, or they
    could not return to it.
That is why the body had to be preserved, or mummified.

The ba returned to the mummy at night.

It was believed the dead traveled to the other world in a boat.

The corpse was buried in a crouching position.
Jars of food were buried with it for use in the new life.

A mummy is a corpse that has been dried out so
  it will not decay.
The earliest Egyptians were mummified naturally.
The corpse was buried in the ground.
The hot dry sand of Egypt dried out the body.
The preserved body turned as hard as stone, into a fossil.

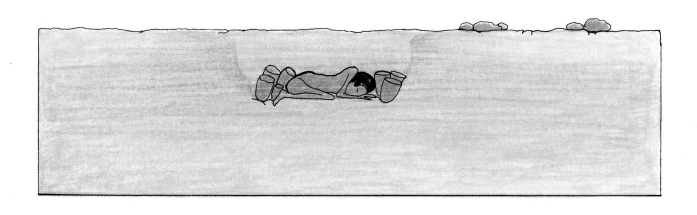

As time went on, burials became more elaborate.
The dead were wrapped in a shroud of cloth or skin.
They were buried in pits lined with wood or stone,
    or in caves.
Bodies not buried directly in the sand became exposed
    to dampness, air, and bacteria.
They decayed.

So people learned how to embalm, or mummify, their dead.
It took centuries of practice to perfect the art.
Embalmers became so expert that the mummies they made
    remained preserved for thousands of years.

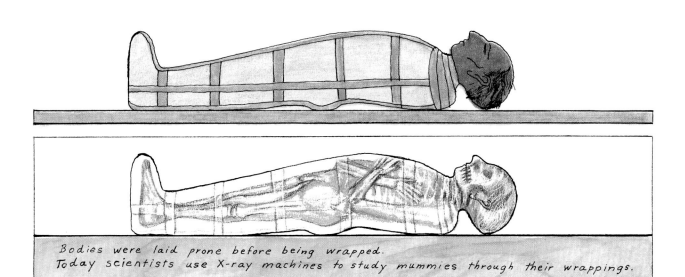

Bodies were laid prone before being wrapped.
Today scientists use X-ray machines to study mummies through their wrappings.

Mummification was a long, complicated, and expensive process.

People were mummified and buried according to what
they could afford.

The poor had modest burials.

Noblemen and others who served the king and his queen
had elaborate burials.

Pharaohs, the kings of Egypt, were the richest of all.

It was believed, too, that a pharaoh became a god
when he died.

So pharaohs were mummified the best and buried in splendor.

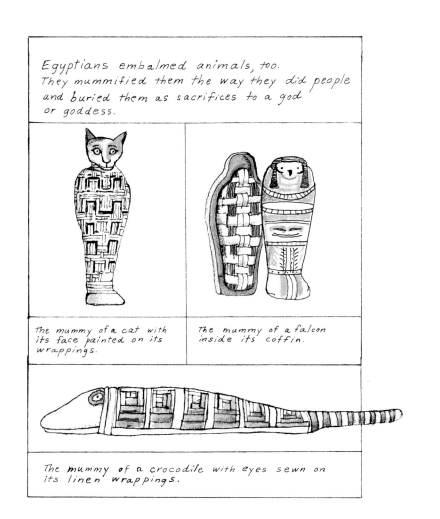

Egyptians embalmed animals, too.
They mummified them the way they did people
and buried them as sacrifices to a god
or goddess.

The mummy of a cat with its face painted on its wrappings.

The mummy of a falcon inside its coffin.

The mummy of a crocodile with eyes sewn on its linen wrappings.

It took seventy days for embalmers to prepare a body.
For a royal or noble burial, embalmers worked in workshops
near the tomb where the mummy would be buried.

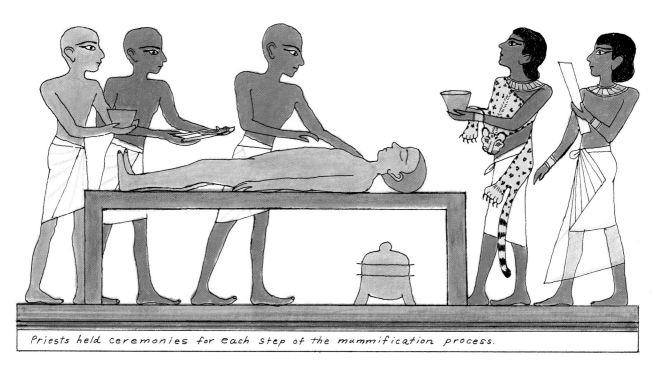

Priests held ceremonies for each step of the mummification process.

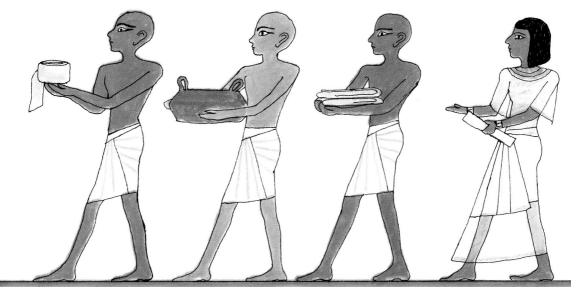

Assistants brought supplies to the embalmers.

Embalmers first took out the inner organs.
They removed the brain through the nostrils with metal hooks.
They made a slit in the left side of the body and took out
   the liver, lungs, stomach, and intestines.
Each of these organs was embalmed in a chemical, natron,
   and put in its own container called a canopic jar.
The heart was left in its place.

In later times, the heart was removed and embalmed, and a stone scarab was put in its place.

Small bundles of natron wrapped in linen were stuffed
   inside the body.
The outside was covered with natron, too.
The chemical dried out the body the same way
   the sand had done.

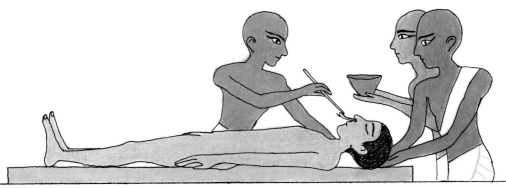

The corpse's brain was removed and probably thrown away.

The inner organs were removed.   The body cavity was stuffed with bundles of natron.

The corpse was placed on a
slanted "embalming bed" with
a groove at the bottom.
It was covered with natron,
a grainy chemical found in
deposits in the Nile River.

Fluids from the corpse dripped
into a container as the
body dried out.

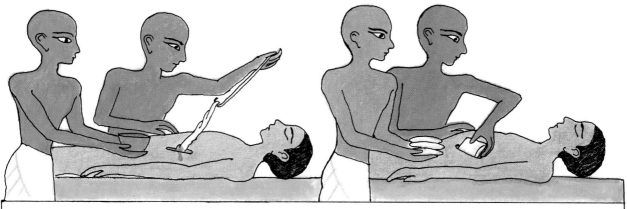

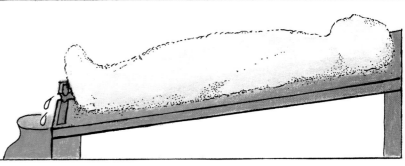

The canopic jars and the gods that guarded them:	HAPY The lungs	DUAMUTEF The stomach	IMSETY The liver	QEBHSENUEF The intestines

The internal organs were mummified separately from the body.
Each organ was wrapped in linen and covered with a mask of the god that protected it.
Then each mummified organ was put into its own canopic jar.
The lid of the jar also bore the image of the god.

The embalming cut was covered with a plate bearing the protective Eye of Horus.

After forty days the natron packs were removed.

The dried, shrunken body was sponged clean and brushed
   with oils, ointments, spices, and resin.

The head and body were stuffed with new packing
   soaked in the same substances.

The eye sockets were plugged with linen and closed.

The nostrils were stuffed with beeswax.

The arms were crossed, and the mummy's fingernails
   and toenails were covered with caps of gold.

The embalming cut was sewn together.

The mummy was adorned with jewels of gold
   and precious stones.

Then the body was carefully bound with long, narrow
    strips of linen.
Fingers, toes, arms, and legs were wrapped individually.
Linen shrouds were placed between the layers of binding,
    and every few layers were glued together with resin.
After twenty layers of shrouds and binding, the mummy's
    body took on its normal size.

It was possible, during the long process, that a piece
    of the corpse—an ear or a toe—would fall off.
This and all leftover material used for the embalming
    were saved in jars to be buried near the tomb.

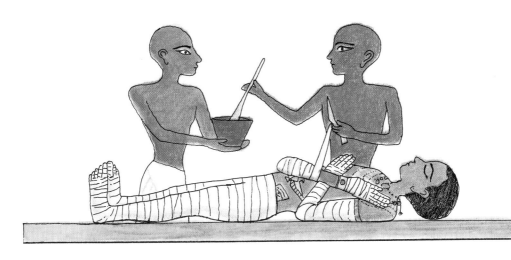

A layer of binding was covered with a shroud. Another layer of binding was placed over that, then another shroud, and so on for twenty layers. The person's name was written on the binding.

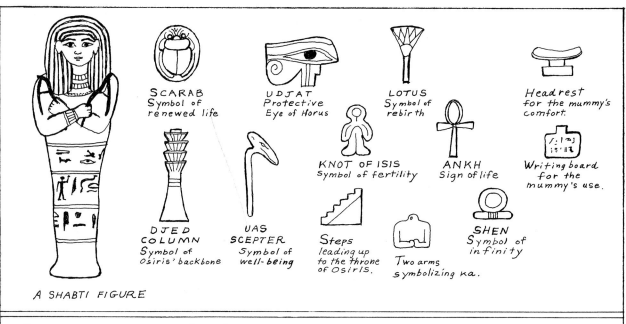

SCARAB
Symbol of
renewed life

UDJAT
Protective
Eye of Horus

LOTUS
Symbol of
rebirth

Headrest
for the mummy's
comfort.

KNOT OF ISIS
Symbol of fertility

ANKH
Sign of life

Writing board
for the
mummy's use.

DJED
COLUMN
Symbol of
Osiris' backbone

UAS
SCEPTER
Symbol of
well-being

Steps
leading up
to the throne
of Osiris.

Two arms
symbolizing ka.

SHEN
Symbol of
infinity

A SHABTI FIGURE

Some of the many amulets found on mummies.
Sometimes hundreds of shabtis were buried with the mummy.

Magical amulets were tucked in between the mummy's wrappings.
The small mummy-shaped figures called *shabtis* held farm tools.
The shabtis would work in the fields of the other world
    for the mummy.

The bound head was covered with a portrait mask.
If anything happened to the mummy, the ba and the ka
    would still be able to recognize it.
The mask, too, was bound.
Then the whole package was wrapped in a shroud
    and given a last coat of resin.
The mummy was finished.

Many portrait masks were made of cartonnage, a material made of linen and plaster. They were molded and painted. Sometimes masks were made of gold and inlaid with precious stones. Often they bore the plaited beard of Osiris.

A collection of spells, called *The Book of the Dead*, was buried with the mummy. The spells, written and illustrated on scrolls of papyrus, were to help the dead find everlasting life.

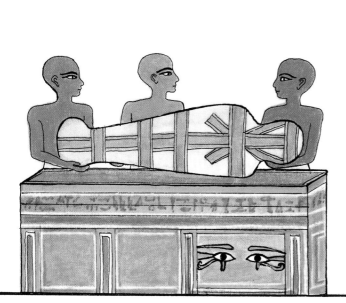

For a period of time mummies were buried on their sides, so that they could look out of the eyes painted on the wooden coffin.

Later, mummies were buried in mummy-shaped coffins made of wood or plaster and painted.

Meanwhile, skilled artists, sculptors, and carpenters
   prepared for the burial.
They made the coffin or a nest of coffins for the mummy.
The coffins were painted inside and out with gods, goddesses,
   and magic spells of protection.

Carpenters prepare a mummiform coffin.

A NEST OF THREE MUMMIFORM COFFINS

The mummy was put into the inner coffin. The inner coffin was covered and placed inside a second covered coffin, which fitted inside an outer coffin. The outer coffin was covered. Eventually, these coffins would be placed into a stone coffin called a sarcophagus.

Magic spells were painted on the coffins in hieroglyphs, the picture writing used by the ancient Egyptians.

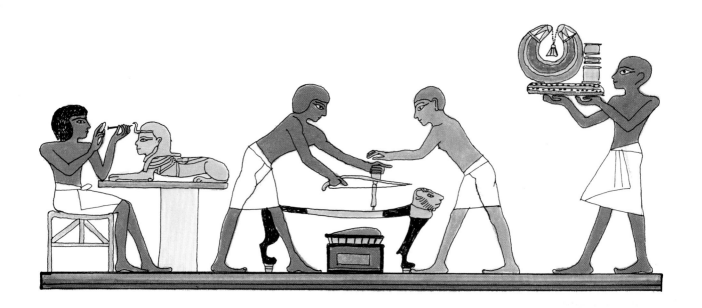

They made jewelry for the mummy and furniture that
  would be buried in the tomb.
They carved statues of the dead person to be placed in the tomb.
These would serve as resting places for the ba and the ka
  should anything happen to the mummy.
A splendid stone sarcophagus was made to hold the coffin.

The walls of the royal tombs were carved and painted
   with scenes that would magically come alive.
The scenes showed the person's new life in the other world.
Dancers and musicians entertained him.
Servants worked in the fields and carried food for him to eat.
The gods and goddesses of the dead welcomed him.

A long, solemn funeral procession took the mummy
   to the tomb.
The mummy rested on an elaborate sled pulled by oxen.
Another sled carried the canopic jars in a chest.

Priests, family, servants, and mourners, who were paid
   to weep, followed.
Porters carried the many possessions that would be buried
   with the mummy.

A tomb was no longer just a pit.
It was a house for the mummy, the ba, and the ka
  that was made to last forever.
A royal tomb was also a fortress against robbers who
  tried to steal mummies and their treasures.

Tombs were more important than houses to Egyptians.
People had them built during their lifetime.
For centuries, the dead were usually buried in tombs
  called mastabas.
Mastabas were made of brick and stone.
Royal mastabas had many storage chambers and were
  beautifully carved and decorated.

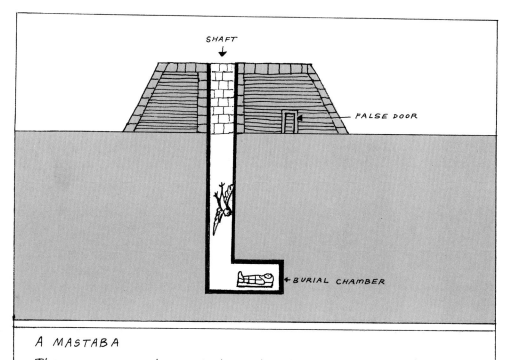

SHAFT

FALSE DOOR

BURIAL CHAMBER

A MASTABA

The mummy was lowered down the shaft to the burial chamber.
It was thought that the ba used the shaft to return to the
mummy at night.
Each tomb had a false door through which the ka
could come and go.

As years went by, pharaohs took more and more with them
   into the tomb.
Tombs became bigger, stronger, and more elaborate.
For a long time pharaohs had pyramids built for themselves.
Pyramids were huge stone monuments that took hundreds
   of workers their lifetime to build.

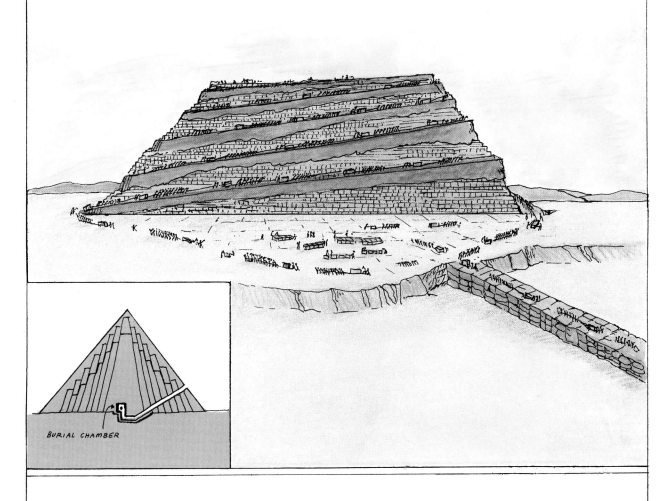

BURIAL CHAMBER

Groups of workers cut and dragged the huge blocks of stone up mud ramps,
starting at each corner of the pyramid. As the pyramid grew, another
ramp was added. It took two million blocks to build a great pyramid.

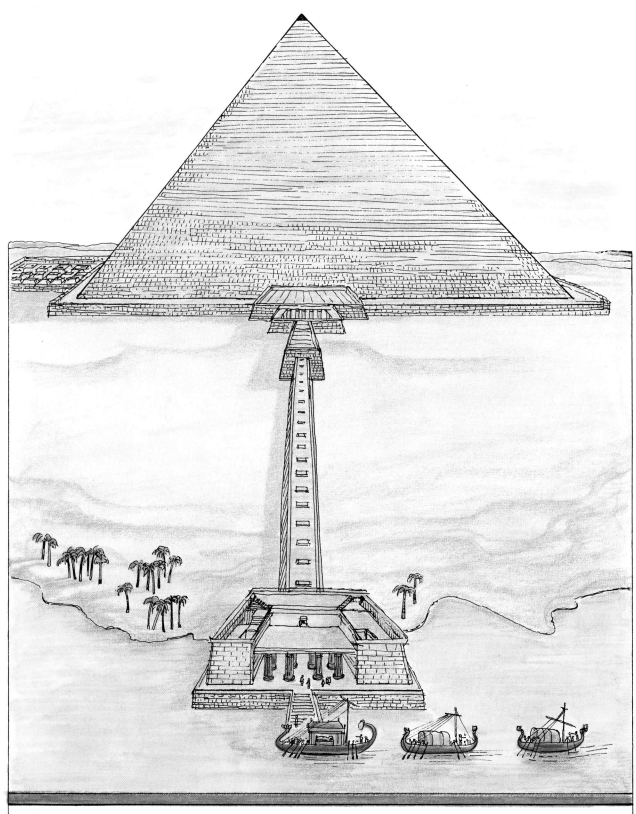

Tombs were built in the desert, where the land could not be farmed.
Sometimes the mourners brought the mummy by boat up the Nile River.
The boat that carried the mummy was buried near the tomb for the
mummy's use in the new life.

The pyramid covered the pharaoh's burial chamber.
Near it were temples, storage chambers, and mastabas
   where the royal family and servants would be buried.
Later, pharaohs were buried in secret underground tombs
   in a deserted place that is known as the Valley of the Kings.
Tunnels, passages, chambers, and the tomb itself were
   cut deep in rock, hidden from sight.
They were magnificently carved and painted.

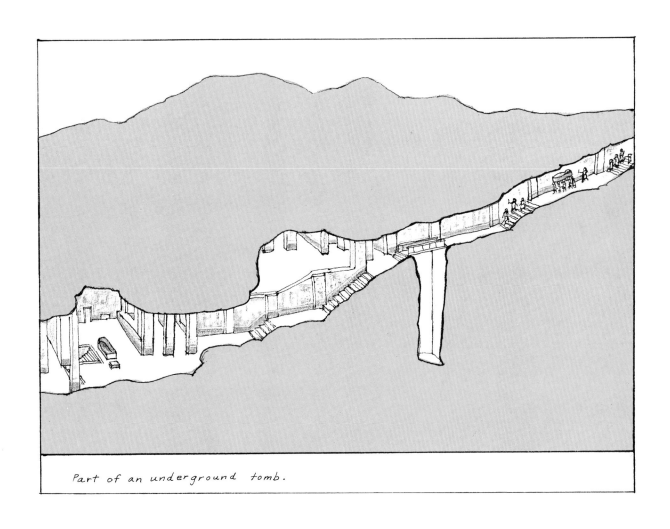

Part of an underground tomb.

A priest dressed as the god Anubis held the mummy up for the ceremony.

The sarcophagus was closed.

The mourners left the tomb for a funeral banquet. The leftover food was buried near the tomb. Thereafter, priests and family worshiped at the temple and brought food offerings to the mummy's ka.

Women wept and threw dust on their heads.

When the funeral procession came to rest at the tomb,
  priests performed a final ritual on the mummy called
  the "Opening of the Mouth."
The mummy's mouth was not actually opened, but magically
  given the ability to speak and eat again.
Then the mummy was put into the sarcophagus, which was
  covered with a heavy stone lid.
The canopic chest, with the jars, guarded by their own gods,
  stood nearby.
The mourners left, and the entrance to the tomb was
  sealed up with a wall of stone slabs.

At last, the mummy was in its eternal resting place
  and on the way to its new life.

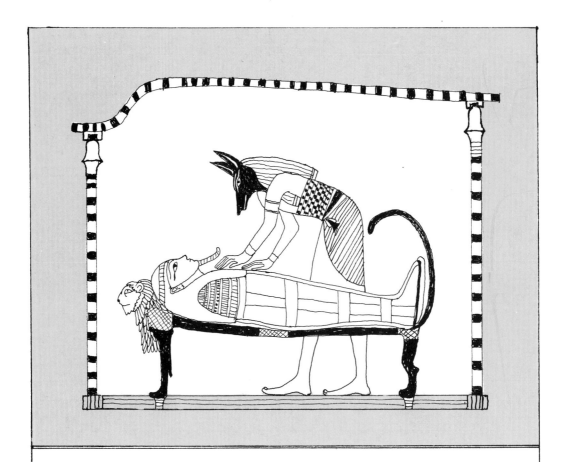

It is said that the first Egyptian to be mummified
   was Osiris, a legendary king.
He was embalmed by Anubis, the jackal god.
When Osiris died, he became a god.
He was King of the Underworld and Prince of the Dead.
It was to Osiris' kingdom the dead wished to go.

Many of the illustrations in this book were adapted from
paintings and sculptures found in ancient Egyptian tombs.